Cartoons by Tim Whyatt
All images ©Tim Whyatt 2002-2017

Published by Studio Press
An imprint of Kings Road Publishing. Part of Bonnier Publishing
The Plaza, 535 King's Road, London, SW10 0SZ

www.bonnierpublishing.co.uk

Printed in Italy   10 9 8 7 6 5 4 3 2 1

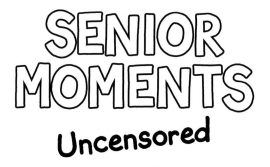

SENIOR MOMENTS
Uncensored

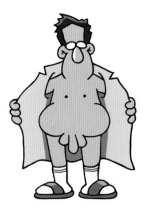

whyatt

BOB FOR APPLES
PIN T
TAIL
THE DO

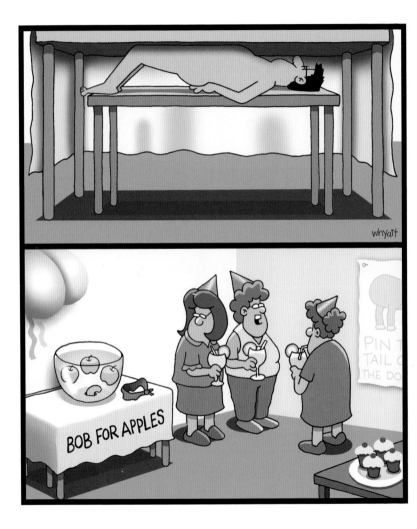

whyatt

BURP
Better out than in
Better in than out
whyatt

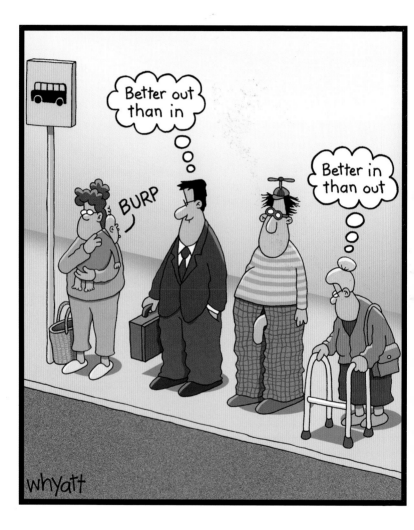

PHOTOS OF YOUR RIDE
whyatt

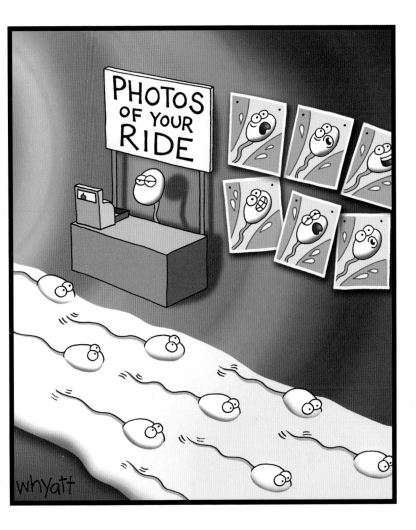

MEET HORNY SINGLES IN YOUR AREA
whyatt

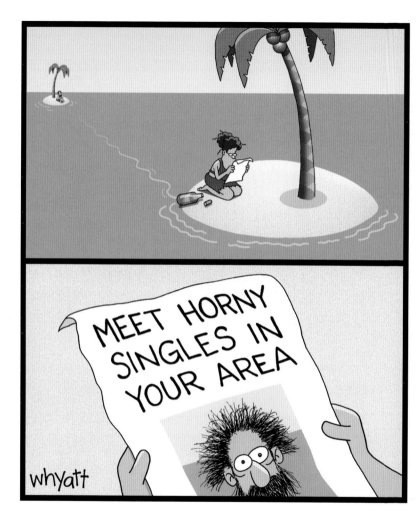

They tend to sag with age but Cyril's learnt to adapt
whyatt

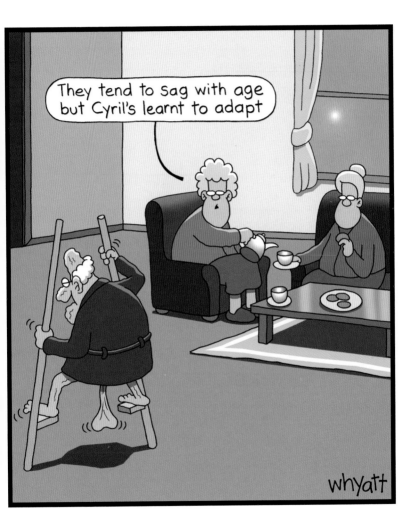

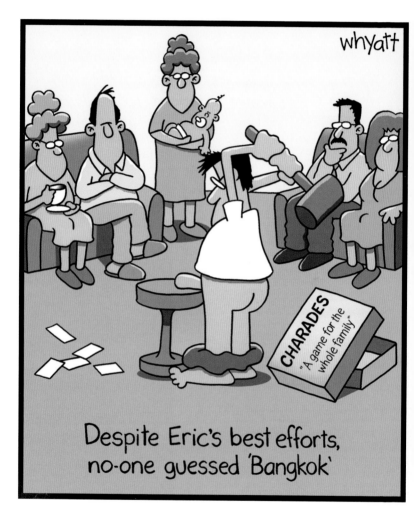

Despite Eric's best efforts,
no-one guessed 'Bangkok'

We need to talk about your duplex with the extended entrance
whyatt

Barry's
BREAST
IMPLANTS
STAFF
PICKS
whyatt

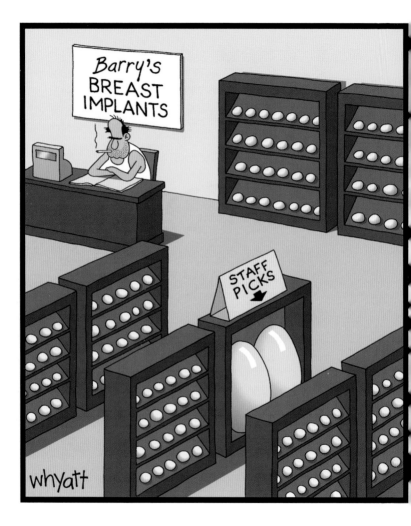

Forget it, Frank, I'm not falling for that again
KISS MY NOSE
whyatt

Where do babies come from?
POP-UP EDITION
whyatt

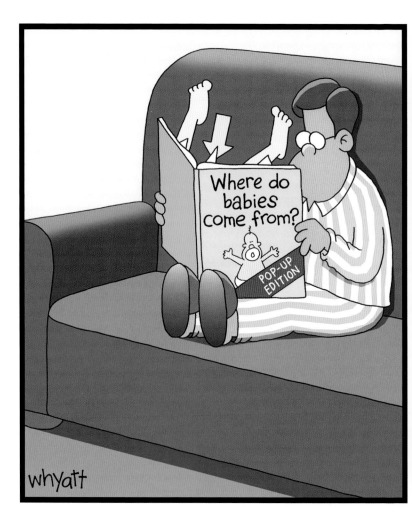

MILF
LILF
whyatt

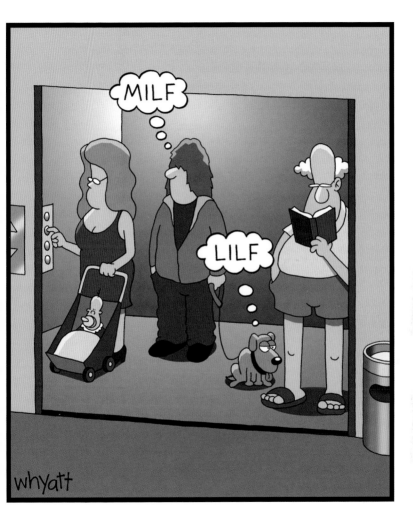

The difference between animals and humans

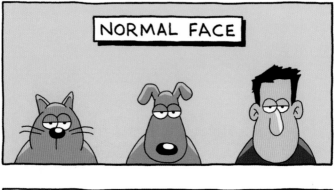

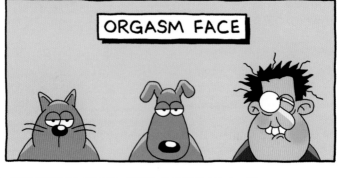

Check this out—
I think the guy
behind us just
got lucky!
whyatt

Big Foot
Big Willy
whyatt

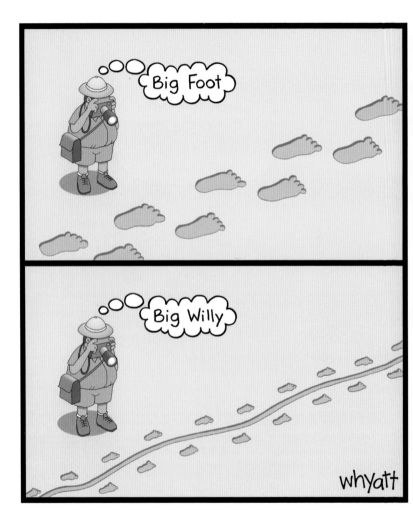

Agnes likes to gaze in to my eyes during sex
whyatt

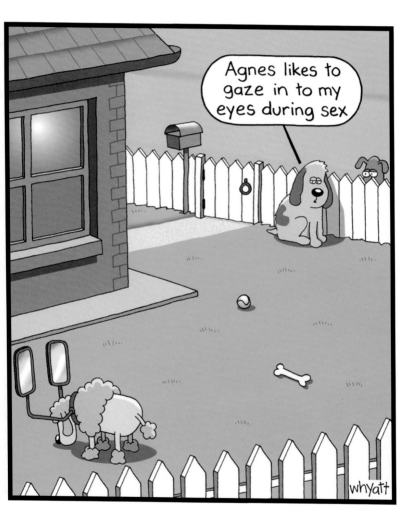

Man, I'd love to be humping a leg right now...
Did I say that out loud?
whyatt

Can't see much, sir —
I think there's a
starfish on the lens
whyatt

Staring up at the ceiling mirror,
Warren couldn't help wondering
if he should grow sideburns

They've been all over her ever since she had that Brazilian Wax
whyatt

whyatt
SOAP
Rubik's
Pube

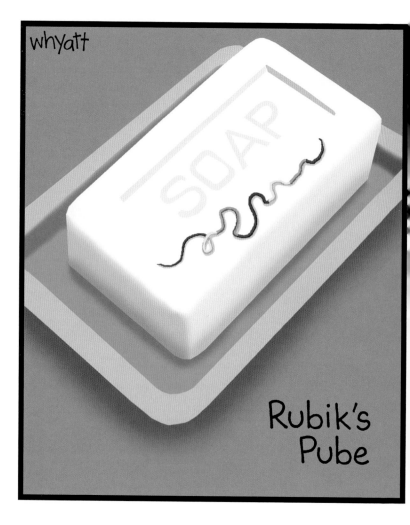

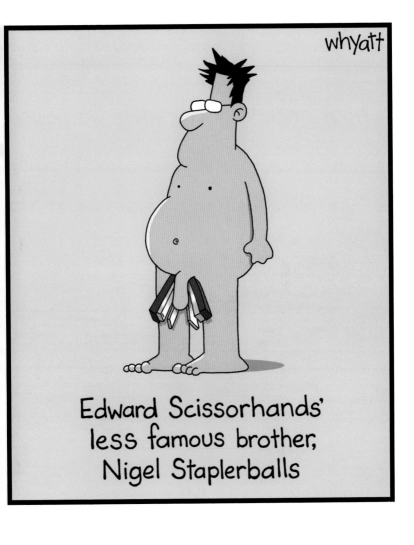

Edward Scissorhands'
less famous brother,
Nigel Staplerballs

Statistics show that 86% of us look at our phone while we poo
whyatt

Congratulations, you've just made it to the top of my shit list
whyatt

Oh good heavens, no, I won't be dancing— I'm just the Door Bitch
SENIOR CITIZENS DANCE NIGHT
whyatt

whyatt
JFK's been shot!

Eric would never forget what he was doing when he heard the news

whyatt
INVENTION OF
THE YEAR AWARDS
Cyril fails to impress the judges
with his "Erection Alarm"

whyatt
Sick puppies

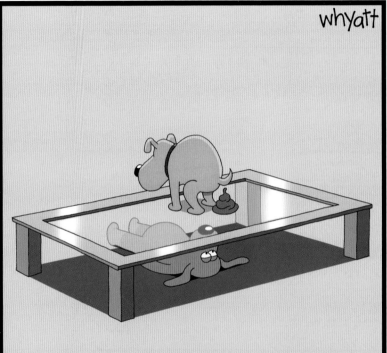

HORNY HANK'S
AUTO REPAIRS
whyatt

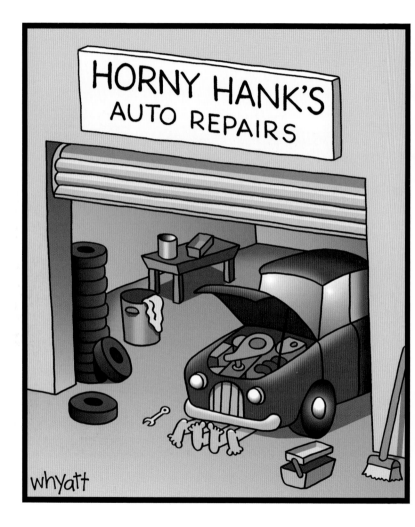

I'll have to call you back, Shirl— Stan's been pestering me for a birthday handjob

WATER TEMPERATURE
whyatt

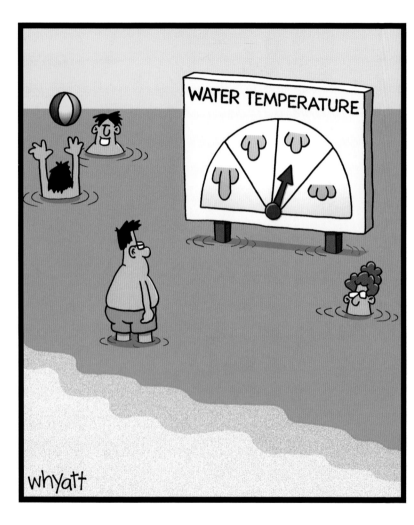

whyatt

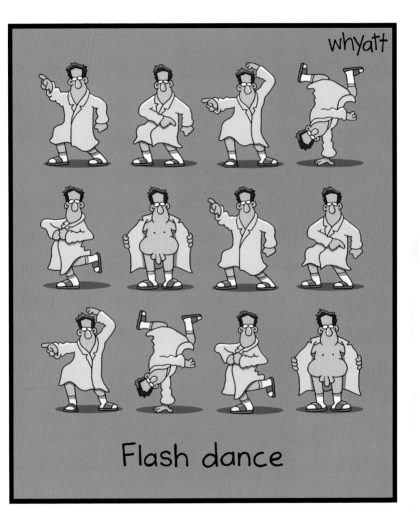

Flash dance

I get a raging boner whenever I think of you
I can't wait to get my hands on your lady lumps
I'll be with you in a minute, Jenkins, I'm just on the phone to my wife

TOOTH FAIRY
TESTICLE FAIRY
whyatt

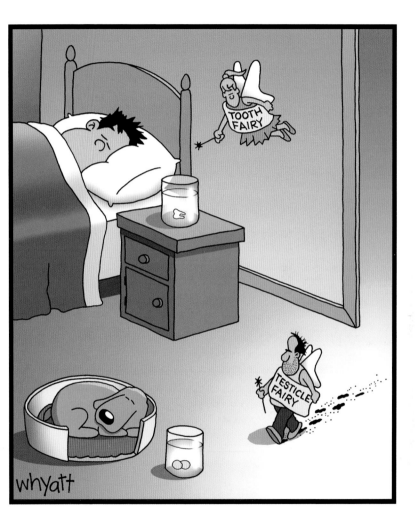

You two-timing bastard!!! Where is she?!
whyatt

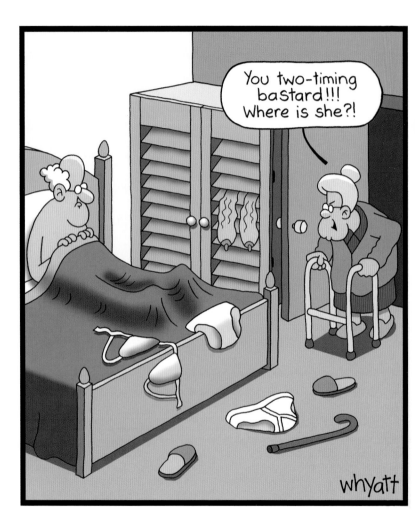

whyatt

The nice young man at the store said you can take it back if it doesn't fit
HAPPY BIRTHDAY
whyatt

whyatt
Come to Papa

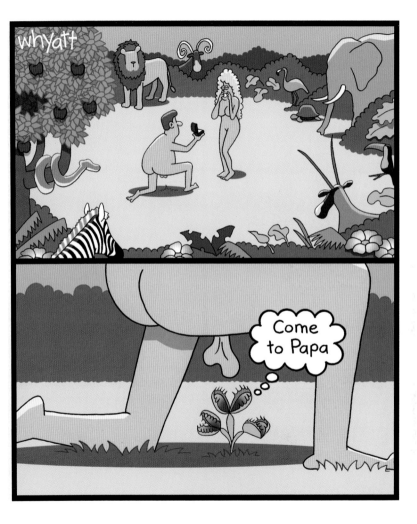

THE STRESS BUSTER 3000
"Go to your Happy Place"
THE STRESS BUSTER 3000
"Go to your Happy Place"
whyatt
"Go to your Happy Place"
"Go to your Happy Place"

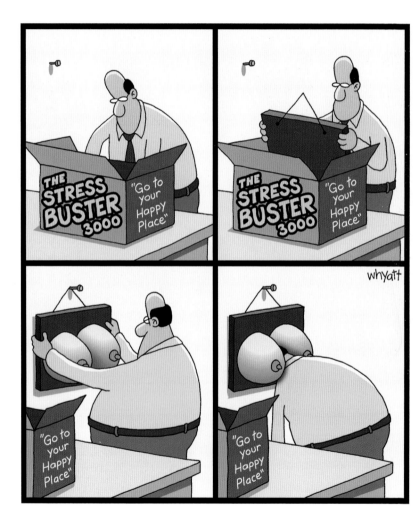

I can't believe you've been stranded here for 30 years! What have you been doing all this time?
whyatt

47TH ANNUAL
BDSM AWARDS
It's an honour just to be dominated
whyatt

whyatt

The Fast & the Furious

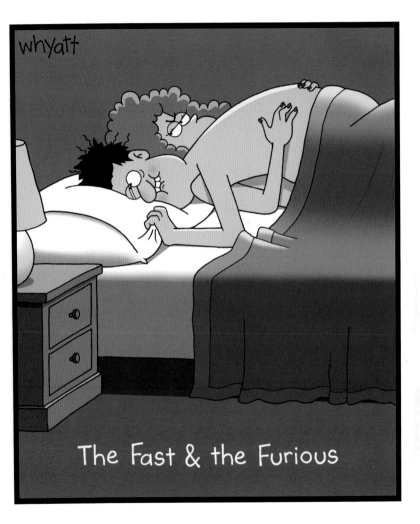

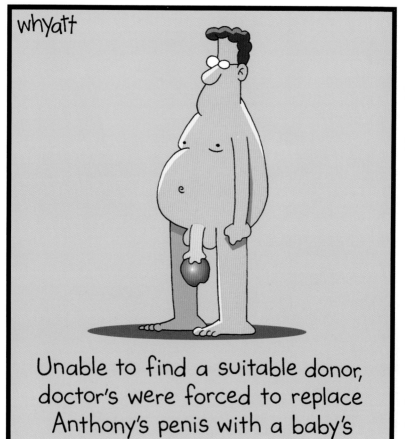

whyatt

Unable to find a suitable donor, doctor's were forced to replace Anthony's penis with a baby's arm holding an apple

Looks like Malcolm's found another one for his collection
whyatt

whyatt
Maybe you should consider moving around occasionally during sex

Scalpel
whyatt
Swab
Adjust junk

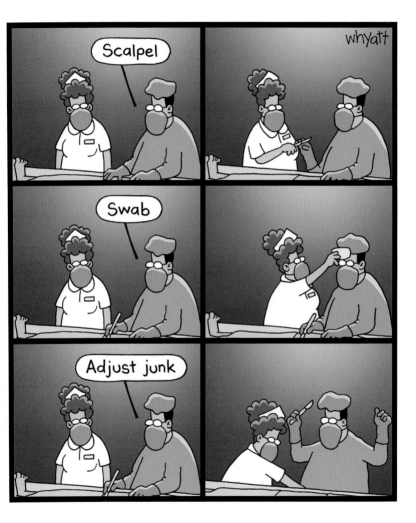